THE BIRKENHEA BUS

TB MAUND FCIT

County Borough of Birkenhead

TRANSPORT DEPARTMENT

Design & Origination: Ian Boumphrey - Desk Top Publisher

Printed by: Eaton Press Ltd Westfield Road Wallasey Merseyside L44 7JB

Published by: Ian & Marilyn Boumphrey
"The Nook"
Acrefield Road
Prenton
Wirral L42 8LD

ISBN 1-899241-00-0

Front Cover: Top - One of Birkenhead's first Leyland Buses on a test run in Leyland before delivery in January 1920.
Bottom - A 1938 Leyland Titan with curvaceous body by Northern Counties of Wigan prepares to leave
Woodside on the Oxton Circle.

PRICE
£5.95

ROUTE DESTINATION NUMBERS AND INDEX.

NEW FERRY AND NEW BRIGHTON   **ROUTE**

	ROUTE
NEW FERRY AND NEW BRIGHTON	
New Ferry and New Brighton	10
Charing Cross and Liscard	11
Charing Cross and Seacombe	12
MORETON.	
*Woodside or Park Station and Moreton Cross	20
*Woodside or Park Station and Bermuda Road	21
*Woodside or Park Station and Moreton Shore	22
*Woodside and Hurrell Road	23
Market Place South and Hurrell Road	24
Market Place South and St. James Church (Via. Conway St.)	25
Moreton (Bermuda Rd.) and New Ferry or Bromborough	26
New Ferry and Hurrell Road	27
EASTHAM, BROMBOROUGH, NEW FERRY	
Woodside and Bromborough Cross	36
Woodside and Allport Road	37
Woodside and Bromborough (Manor Road)	38
Woodside and Eastham Village	40
Bromborough and Upton	43
Central Station and St. Paul's Road	45
Charing Cross and Bromborough	47
New Ferry and Charing Cross and Upton	48
Woodside and New Ferry	49
OLD CHESTER ROAD, PORT SUNLIGHT, LR. BEBINGTON	
*Woodside or Central Station and Lower Bebington	50
Claughton Village and Port Sunlight	51
Park Station and Port Sunlight	52
Charing Cross and Port Sunlight	53
Central Station and Town Lane or Bebington Station	55
Charing Cross and Bebington Show Ground	56
Bidston Road and Port Sunlight	57
TRANMERE AND HR. BEBINGTON	
*Woodside and Heath Rd. (Via Whetstone Lane & Church Rd.)	60
*Woodside, Central Station, Kings Road and Village Road (Via Borough Road)	63
*Woodside, Kings Road and New Ferry (Via Borough Road)	64
Central Station and Bebington Road (Via Whetstone Lane and Church Road)	65
*Woodside and Thornton Road (Via. Whetstone Lane)	66
Central Station and Thornton Road (Via. Whetstone Lane)	67
ARROWE, IRBY & THURSTASTON	
*Woodside and Prenton Dell Road	70
*Woodside and Heswall	71
*Woodside, Irby and Thurstaston	72
*Woodside and Irby	73
Central Station and Irby	74
*Woodside and Arrowe Park	75
Central Station and Arrowe Park	76
*Woodside and Prenton, Arrowe, Upton and Moreton	77
*Woodside and Greasby (via Arrowe Park)	78
Market Place South and Storeton Road (Birch Road)	79
PRENTON	
*Woodside and Prenton Lane (War Memorial)	80
Central Station and Prenton Lane (Storeton Road)	81
*Woodside and Singleton Avenue	82
*Woodside and Prenton Lane (Storeton Road)	83
*Woodside and Thornton Road (Storeton Road)	84
NORTH CIRCLE (via Claughton Road)	90
Market Place South and Cemetery Gates (via. Claughton Rd.)	91
Woodside and St. James' Church (via. Claughton Road)	92
NORTH CIRCLE (via Cleveland Street)	94
Woodside and Station Road (via Cleveland Street)	95
OXTON CIRCLE (via Conway Street)	2
Woodside and Upton Road	3
Woodside and Laird Street	4
OXTON CIRCLE (via Borough Road)	6
Woodside and Laird Street Depot	7
UPTON	
Upton and Bromborough	43
Park Station and Upton	15
Park Station and Arrowe Park	16
Special Buses to Planters only	O.O.
Special Buses to Lairds, Green Lane Entrance	99

Certain part-journey services will not carry route numbers.

*Approach Woodside via. Argyle Street and Hamilton Square Station.
Leave via. Hamilton Square Station and Hamilton Street.

Taken from a 1941 Birkenhead Corporation Transport Time Table.

INTRODUCTION

When the first purpose-built street tramway was opened between Woodside ferry and Birkenhead Park on 30th August 1860, Birkenhead reserved for itself a special place in local transport history. Three horse-drawn tramway companies eventually ran four routes and then, at the turn of the century, the Corporation bought the tramways and adopted electric power. The network of routes, extending from Woodside to New Ferry, Higher Tranmere, Prenton, Shrewsbury Road, Park Road South, Laird Street and along the Line of Docks formed the mainstay of the town's public transport system for the next thirty years. In the early days, there were ambitious plans for tramways to Greasby, Frankby and West Kirby and even from New Ferry and Eastham Ferry to Chester but the future lay with the motor bus.

The Town Council had already obtained Parliamentary powers to run motor buses in July 1914 and, on the eve of the outbreak of World War I in August had hired a London bus and gone on a jaunt to Moreton. However, although the war prevented any immediate progress being made, the military needs accelerated the technical evolution of motor vehicles, resulting in the 1919 buses being more rugged and reliable than those of 1914.

The first Corporation buses ran on routes designed to compete with the tramways as little as possible and to feed passengers to the loss-making steamers at Rock Ferry. Progress was steady with Birkenhead's buses soon running out to Moreton and Upton and, in 1925, the Council took what was then a bold decision by replacing the trams running along Claughton Road and Park Road South by motor buses which ran beyond the former terminus along Tollemache Road to Flaybrick Hill Cemetery and St. James' Church. This was the first such changeover on Merseyside.

Trams continued to run on the other routes but the network of bus routes expanded so rapidly that in the year 1928-29, the buses carried almost a million passengers more than the trams. In 1930, after lengthy negotiations, Birkenhead Corporation and Crosville made an agreement which enabled the latter's buses to run through from the outskirts of the town to Woodside in return for the Corporation's buses being allowed to run out to Bromborough, Eastham, Thurstaston, Frankby and Heswall. The New Ferry trams were scrapped in 1931, Tranmere and Prenton in 1934, Line of Docks in 1935 and, finally, the Oxton and Claughton Circle on 17th July 1937.

In the 1930s, Birkenhead possessed a highly efficient bus system with frequent services to all parts of the town and neighbouring districts. The war tested the Transport Department to the limit but services were maintained despite the air raids which devastated part of the Laird Street depot, killing several employees. After the war, there was a travel boom, over 78 million passengers being carried over seven million miles in the year 1949-50. During those times, almost everyone travelled by bus at cheap fares which had been stable since the early 1930s. Thereafter costs and fares rose and there was a gradual decline as private car ownership increased and social habits changed following the introduction of television.

By 1969, the number of passenger-journeys had fallen to little more than half - 41 million over 5.9 million miles and, on 1st December 1969 the Birkenhead Transport undertaking was merged with those of Liverpool and Wallasey under the control of the Merseyside Passenger Transport Executive. Gradually the proud blue buses disappeared in favour of a bland livery described as verona green and jonquil. In October 1986, regulation of bus services was abolished and since then buses of many hues have filled the town's streets - but that is another story.

1 Horse-drawn omnibuses started to run between Woodside and Oxton in 1848 and there were few improvements in design for the next 40 years. Passengers sat facing each other in the cramped saloon and others were accommodated back-to-back on a 'knifeboard' seat outside. The outside passengers usually paid a lower fare. A 'trace horse' was often attached to assist on the steeper gradients.
Courtesy R.L. Wilson

2 Surviving records reveal that the Upton bus was first licensed on 11th March 1891 but nothing more is known. It is seen in Claughton Village in 1895. The climb from the village to the waterworks and up Ford Hill must have been a severe trial for the horses.
Courtesy T.G. Turner

3   New Chester Road in the early years of the twentieth century with the New Ferry-Bromborough omnibus. This was a 'garden seat' bus with pairs of seats on the upper deck, a refinement dating from the 1880s. The Bromborough service was started in 1898 by the Wirral Tramway Co. as an extension of their tram route from Woodside. It was taken over for a time by the Birkenhead United Tramways & Omnibus Co. but that company, renamed the Birkenhead Carriage Co. went into receivership in 1902 and the buses were then run by the Oxton Carriage Co. Ltd from stables at 87 Church Road, Higher Tranmere. The company's initials can be seen on the driver's apron. The picture is taken outside 312 New Chester Road.
Courtesy T.G. Turner

4   The last horse bus service in Birkenhead was run by Thomas Peters, described as a 'cocoa rooms proprietor' of 181 Price Street. It started on 7th September 1903 using second-hand 20-seat buses bought from the bankrupt Birkenhead Carriage Co. Note that access to the upper deck seats is by rope ladders. The buses ran from Seacombe Ferry to Charing Cross via the Four Bridges, Watson Street and Exmouth Street from stables in Back Menai Street and Watson Street and other premises at 2-4 Devonshire Road which had been used for many years by Birkenhead's principal bus operator, Alderman Thomas Evans. His initials 'T.E 1853' can still be seen on the gable. This service ran until after the 1914-18 War being replaced by motor buses of the Birkenhead Motor Works until Corporation buses took over in 1921.

5

5a

5-5a The Mersey Railway Co. believed, with some justification, that the Corporation tramway service to Central Station was inferior to that to Woodside ferry and put on their own bus service between Central Station and Slatey Road via Grange Road from 11th December 1905. It was soon extended to Bidston Road and then made into a circular route with alternate buses running via Oxton Road, Balls Road, Christchurch Road, Village Road and Wellington Road. On Sundays the buses ran trips to the Glegg Arms at Gayton and Heswall. Legal action by Birkenhead Corporation stopped the service on 17th March 1906 but a new service between Rock Ferry Station and Port Sunlight started on 16th May 1907. The House of Lords ruled that the railway company had no powers to run buses and the service ceased on 8th July 1907.

6   Advertisement from a Birkenhead Corporation Timetable - August 1932.

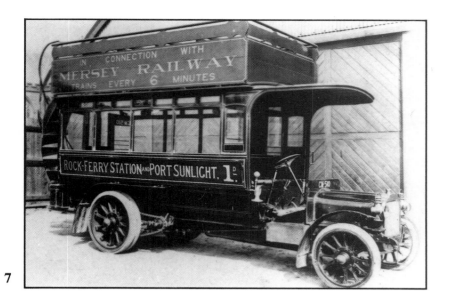

7

7-8 The Mersey Railway Co. had 10 buses - all chain-driven Saurers with 34-seat open-top bodies supplied by the Motor Car Emporium Ltd. of Shepherd Bush registered CM 501-10. They were kept in a garage on railway land in Argyle Street South.
Courtesy J. Cummings

8

9 The Port Sunlight service originally ran along New Chester Road, Bolton Road and Wood Street but after trouble with Higher Bebington Urban District Council who objected to Sunday buses, a licence was obtained to run also by way of Dacre Hill, Old Chester Road and Greendale Road on weekdays only. This poster was issued to announce the start of the Circular Route on 29th May 1907.
Courtesy R.L. Wilson

9

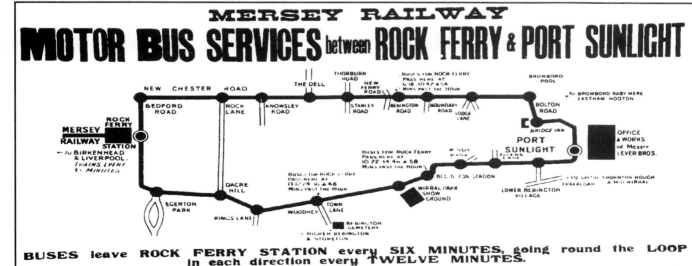

GREAT WESTERN RAILWAY.

Motor Omnibus Service

BETWEEN

LIVERPOOL & BIRKENHEAD

(WOODSIDE STATION)

EACH WEEK-DAY,

FOR THE CONVEYANCE OF

Passengers, Luggage, and Parcels

To and from the Great Western Railway Express Trains running between Birkenhead and Chester, Shrewsbury, Wolverhampton. Birmingham, London, South Wales, and the West of England.

10-11   The first cross-river bus service was run by the Great Western Railway to convey tourists between Liverpool hotels and Woodside Station. The Ferries department allowed the bus to have 'pole position' on the luggage boat (vehicle ferry) to avoid delay and the picture shows Milnes-Daimler bus AX 123 driving on to the boat at Liverpool landing stage. The service lasted for only three months from 20th September 1909. The three buses were kept on Corporation land south of Woodside station and parties could be picked up at their homes by special arrangement.

Courtesy J. Cummings

12   Early in 1919, Birkenhead Corporation ordered 10 Leyland 'O' type buses with 40-48hp engines and 32-seat bodies at a cost of £1,317 each. Alterations were made to the depots to house six at New Ferry and four at Laird Street. The first service started on 12th July 1919 between Rock Ferry pier and Park Station via Bedford Avenue, Bebington Road, Derby Road, Charing Cross and Park Road East. After more buses had been delivered, the route was extended to Moreton Cross on 30th August. Bus No. 3 is seen at Charing Cross; the paper destination label reads 'Duke St. & Rock Ferry Pier via Derby Road'. For a time these buses ran on benzole, a less refined product than petrol, giving a consumption of 9 mpg.
Leyland

13   In 1921, the Corporation bought two second-hand AEC 'B' type buses from the London General Omnibus Co. The B type had proved very successful in London and in France during the 1914-18 war. Although the output of its 5.3 litre swept volume engine was less than that of a mini, it was designed to pull well at low speeds. These buses were re-registered CM 1711-12 (Nos.11-12) and ran in Birkenhead, mainly to Moreton until 1925-26 after which they were sold and converted to lorries.
AEC

14

15

14-15   Five two-year old Straker-Squire buses were bought from Plymouth Corporation in 1922 followed by a similar vehicle (which is said to have been a cancelled order) from a local dealer and charabanc proprietor, W.B. 'Barney' Horn. Two of the Plymouth buses were dismantled for spares, a shrewd move as it turned out, because Strakers went into liquidation in 1925. The others became Nos. 13-15 while the Horn bus was 16. The latter is seen in both these views, (above) at Raby Mere (then a popular venue for church outings) in company with Harding's Daimler Y charabanc CM 4406 and (below) after sale to the Corporation at Rock Ferry on the Moreton route. No. 16 was blue when it arrived and was not repainted until 1924. Rock Ferry was popular with trippers many of whom can be seen on the ferry pier. After withdrawal in 1927, No. 13 became an experimental street-sweeper and No. 14 a tower-wagon.   *Courtesy T.G. Turner*

16   In February 1923, the Corporation bought a small Thornycroft 'B' type with 20-seat Strachan and Brown body, designed for one-man operation, which became No. 17. It had a change dispensing machine and the folding door was controlled by the driver by means of a lever. It was first used between Charing Cross, Park Station and Upton which was not a profitable route as the Corporation was trying to combat competition from Crosville. In 1925 it was transferred to be the first 'Shopping Bus' which started on 12th June 1925 between Market Place South and the top of Oxton Road via Grange Road but was latterly used between Moreton Cross and the Shore, being withdrawn in 1928. Its registration letters were 'CM' not 'CN' as shown in this touched-up picture.   *John I Thornycroft*

17   In the early days of motor buses, Councils took pride in having their fleets photographed professionally from time to time. This Sunday morning line-up was in Park Road North, between Cavendish Road and Mallaby Street, a section on which the tram track was never used for a regular service.
Leyland

Advertisement taken from Birkenhead Corporation Tramways and Motors Timetables August 1932.

18

18-18a From 1923, Birkenhead Corporation standardised on Leyland buses except where special types were required. The six G7 models put on the road that year were very similar to the original buses of 1919 but a little shorter as many towns would not license buses longer than 25 ft. They had solid tyres and front wheels of smaller diameter to ease steering. Later they were fitted with new wheels, mudguards and pneumatic tyres, giving them something of a limousine look. The lower view shows No. 19 at Prenton tram terminus, Prenton Road West with wire mesh over the windows during the General Strike in May 1926 when buses were operated with volunteer crews and a police escort.

Courtesy T.G. Turner

18a

19

The Cross, Moreton.

20

19-20 The six ugly, box-like Leyland GH7s which arrived in 1924 appeared to be longer than the G7s but were of exactly the same dimensions, the illusion being created by the absence of a long bonnet. Seats for 40 passengers were crammed into them. Pneumatic tyres were fitted later though No. 25 had them on the front wheels only. No. 29 was one of two reseated to 39 and was the subject of early spray-painting experiments. The lower picture shows what is believed to be No. 26 at Moreton Cross with the Plough Inn in the centre of the picture. After withdrawal in 1930, these buses were converted into lorries.

Leyland Motors/Courtesy T.G. Turner

21 The Thornycroft was assisted on the 'Shopping Bus' by this strange Guy 'J' 20-seat runabout of a type popular on sea-front services in various resorts. The bus stopped anywhere by request along Grange Road and the small-diameter wheels were designed to give easy access for housewives laden with shopping. The route was soon extended to the Half Way House, Storeton Road and, in 1930, to Birch Road. For a time a halfpenny fare was charged for short rides along Grange Road.
T.B.Maund Collection

22

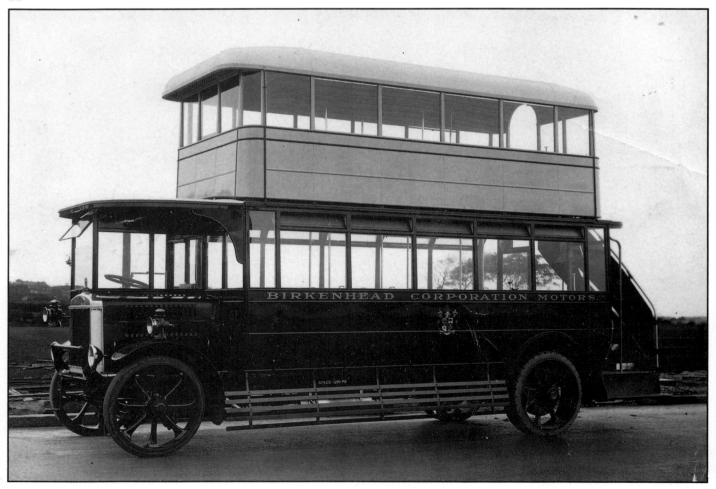

22-24   Birkenhead's first covered-top double-deck buses were Leyland Leviathans, a new model in 1925 of which Birkenhead took the first eight built. At this stage, tyre technology had not advanced to the state where vehicles of this weight could be fitted with pneumatic tyres but the early Leviathans were eventually so equipped on the front axle only as shown in the view of No. 45 of a second batch of ten delivered in 1926. The rear of No. 37 is shown crossing the old Duke Street swing bridge. The service from Charing Cross to Seacombe started on 19th March 1921 with Birkenhead and Wallasey buses working early and late shifts alternately. A summer service to Harrison Drive was run by Birkenhead buses in 1921-23 and the Liscard route started on 24th October 1921 after which each Corporation worked each route on alternate weeks.
Leyland/Courtesy T.G. Turner

23

24

25

26

25-26   An improved version of the Leviathan appeared in 1927 and Birkenhead bought another 10, bringing their fleet up to 28. Only 93 Leviathans were built and 40 of them saw service in Wirral, the other 12 being used by Crosville on the West Kirby and New Ferry-Bromborough services. The 1927 buses originally had solid tyres but were soon equipped with pneumatics all round. They were unusual in having enclosed staircases, a feature which did not become general for another three years. Their 55-seat capacity made them popular on the Woodside-Moreton services where 100 passengers were sometimes carried on summer Sundays to and from the Shore where three Leviathans are seen. Route numbers were adopted from 1st January 1931. The lower view is of the terminus at Bermuda Road, Moreton showing one of the early Leviathans (No. 31) and a Leyland Titan. The difference in height of the two models is clearly discernible.
Courtesy T.G. Turner

27

27a

27-27a   In 1926, three Guy 'BB' buses were purchased, mainly for the Shopping Bus route. Their 27 seats were arranged partly facing forward and partly longitudinally in order to satisfy a police objection to buses more than 6ft 9in wide running along Grange Road. It says much for the economics of bus manufacture of the time that the makers were prepared to produce non-standard vehicles for such a small order. These buses were the first to have pneumatic tyres fitted from new but they had a short life in Birkenhead being sold in 1930.
Motor Transport

28

28-28a/b Earlier Leyland single-deck buses had been based on goods models with straight chassis but the Leyland Lion which came on stream in 1926 was the first designed as a passenger vehicle with a lower floor level. Birkenhead bought 14 of the long-wheelbase model PLSC3, seating 36 passengers. No. 69 is seen at Bermuda Road, Moreton on the Rock Ferry service, No. 66 with proud driver at Birch Road after route number boxes had been fitted and another at Arrowe Park in company with a Leviathan, G7 No. 20 (by then fitted with pneumatics) and a Crosville bus. The occasion is the World Scout Jamboree in July-August 1929. *D.S. Deacon/T.G. Turner/P.E.Wright (Courtesy T.G. Turner)*

28a

28b

29 The low-height Leyland Titan TD1 revolutionised bus design with a low step and a side gangway on the upper deck giving access to alternate rows of three or four seats. This gangway protruded into the lower saloon where passengers on the offside were advised to lower their heads when leaving their seats. The overall height was just over 13 ft., low enough to pass comfortably under Chester Street and Bebington Station bridges which were impassable to Leviathans. The early Titans in 1928, of which No. 93 is shown, had an open staircase under which a spare wheel was stored and single line destination indicator at the front only. After receiving its first 10 Titans, Birkenhead was so impressed that it replaced a repeat order for Lions with a second Titan order; these five buses had twin route indicators front and rear. All the open-staircase Titans were enclosed by Massey Bros. of Wigan in 1933 and ran until 1938.
Massey Bros

30 A rear-end comparison of the open and enclosed versions of the Leyland Titan showing one of the first batch and No. 96 of the first enclosed batch of 1929, loading outside Woodside railway station. Note the hackney-carriage licence number which was due to disappear with the advent of national public service vehicle licensing in 1931.
Courtesy T.G. Turner/ Leyland

31 The enclosed version of the Leyland Titan TD1 was to become the standard Birkenhead bus, no fewer than 62 being purchased in 1929-31, the last of which remained in service until early 1947. No.96, fitted with the side destination indicators which became standard, was photographed soon after delivery in April 1929.
Courtesy T.G. Turner/Leyland

32

32-32a/b   The new Titans facilitated a big expansion of bus services in 1928-30. From 1st August 1930, Corporation buses took over the Bromborough and Eastham routes from Crosville and two months later, the Woodside-Heswall route via Irby and Thurstaston. The Express buses ran in from Eastham, Heswall and Moreton in the mornings and outward to Moreton in the evening peak. Other buses on the longer routes had minimum fares to discourage short distance passengers. The Prenton (via Singleton Avenue) route started on 14th July 1928, terminating at Osmaston Road until it was extended to Prenton Dell Road in October 1930. The Lower Bebington (via Old Chester Road) service was introduced on 3rd March 1929 at the request of Bebington Council. The Kings Road (via Higher Tranmere) service at first ran only to the borough boundary at Cavendish Drive but was extended to Kings Lane (1930), Village Road (1934), Gorsey Hey (1935), Pulford Road (1937) and Cross Lane (1945).

Leyland

32a

32b

33-34 In 1929, Leyland replaced the PLSC range of Lions by a completely redesigned model coded LT and in 1930 the Corporation purchased six LT2s with rear entrances and 35 seats, to replace the obsolescent single-deck buses of the mid-1920s. Single-deck buses were also needed for the route under the railway bridge in Bromborough Road, Trafalgar. No. 129 is seen when new in the Haymarket, the departure point of the Shopping Bus. The lower view shows a Lion awaiting passengers from the Rock Ferry boat in company with one of the second batch of open-staircase Titans on the Rock Ferry-Moreton service No. 26. During the war, four of them were converted to perimeter seating which facilitated a large number of standees.

D.S. Deacon/commercial post-card

33

34

35

35 The later Titans dispensed with the 'passing places' in the upper-deck gangway, all the rows except the rear one having four seats; this increased the capacity from 48 to 51. The petrol-engined buses which remained during the war had their cream parts painted black and No. 136 is seen in this condition towards the end of its days. The 95 route was a part-way of the North Circle No. 94, running at peak hours between Woodside and Station Road or St. James' Church via Cleveland Street and Beaufort Road.

TG Turner

36. In 1931, the PSV (Construction and Use) Regulations were changed and two-axle double-deck buses could be 26 ft long instead of 25 ft. Leyland produced the Titan TD2 which, although of similar appearance to the TD1, was a foot longer and had a more powerful engine - 7.6 litres instead of 6.8. No. 164 was the first of seven TD2s new in May 1932, the last two of which (169-70) were the first diesel-engined buses in the Birkenhead fleet. Nos. 164 and 167 were among 9 buses converted to producer-gas operation, generated in two-wheel trailers, during the 1939-45 war.
Leyland

37 The 1933 Titan TD2s (176-84) were all powered by 8.6 litre diesel engines and were the first to have moquette seating. The body of No. 182 was destroyed in an air raid and it was rebodied by East Lancs. Coachbuilders in 1942. No. 183 lost its body in a fire in January 1936 and was converted to a breakdown vehicle seen here dealing with No. 179 in post-war days.
T.G. Turner collection

38 Perhaps to keep Leyland Motors on their toes, Birkenhead bought seven Daimler CH6 buses with Massey bodies, two in 1931 and five in 1932. They had fluid flywheels and were generally regarded as under-powered; they were all withdrawn and sold in 1938. No. 158 is seen at Seacombe ferry with the top of a Wallasey tram in the background. *D.S. Deacon* **38**

39 The last petrol-engined bus to be taken into the Birkenhead Corporation fleet was No. 185, one of only 23 AEC 'Q' type double-deckers built. The engine was mounted vertically behind the front axle which was further back than usual. The Birkenhead Q was the only low-height example, its 60-seat body being built by MCCW. This unusual bus arrived in July 1933 and was the first to be painted in the blue livery which became standard for many years. It is seen unloading passengers outside the Capitol cinema at Liscard with a Wallasey tram in the background. It was withdrawn in June 1940, sold for only £200 and ran until 1949 for T. Worth, an Oxfordshire operator who collected a number of second-hand AEC Qs. **39**
AEC

40 The last low-height buses to be bought by Birkenhead Corporation were three Leyland Titan TD3c's which went into service when the Prenton and Tranmere trams were replaced by buses on 1st October 1934. They had NCME all-metal bodies built to Leyland designs. The TD3 was the first model to have the long radiator and the 'c' suffix indicated that they were fitted with hydraulic torque-convertors instead of the normal transmission. The words 'Gearless Bus' were shown on the radiator, the device being marketed as especially suitable for ex-tram drivers. Titan No. 87 had been fitted experimentally with the first torque convertor, of Swedish design, in 1933 and this type of transmission was fitted to all subsequent deliveries of new buses in Birkenhead up to 1939. No. 187 is seen in Port Sunlight on a workers' journey off the normal 27 route which was a part-way service on the Bromborough-Moreton (26) service. *Courtesy T.G. Turner*

41

41a

41-41a/b Thirty buses of this general design went into service in 1934-36 though there were three design variations and two bodybuilders - Massey and Northern Counties, both of Wigan. They were the first high-bridge buses since the Leviathans. The 1934 buses (189-97) had the front route number moved from the upper deck windows into the bodywork but no route number at the rear; the 1935 delivery (198-207) had a similar layout front and rear as shown in the post-war view of 199 at Laird Street depot while the 1936 batch (208-18) introduced the larger route numbers beside the destination display which remained standard for the next 33 years. Nine of these buses were damaged in air raids and four had new bodies fitted, mainly in 1942. No. 211 of the last batch is pictured when new on route 80 which replaced the Prenton trams. At first this route ran round a loop formed by Woodchurch Lane, Storeton Road and Prenton Road West but, in October 1937, it was extended to the War Memorial in Prenton Lane.

J.P. Williams/ T.G.Turner/ T.Lawson

41b

42

42a

42-42a   The last trams ran on the Oxton and Claughton Circle route on 17th July 1937 and on the following day 40 new Leyland Titan TD5c buses with Massey bodies were placed in service. When new they had white roofs as shown but they became grey during the war to make them less conspicuous to enemy aircraft and were painted blue after the war. No. 224 stands at Woodside working the anti-clockwise North Circle with No. 273 of 1938. A further 10 buses to the same design were delivered in 1938. No. 221 is shown at The Wiend, the terminus of routes 66 (from Woodside) and 67 (from Central Station) which were part-way routes on the No. 60 service (the present-day 64A). Note the typical Corporation bus stop sign; these retained the chocolate and cream livery long after the buses were painted blue.

T.Lawson/T. Davies (Courtesy T.G. Turner)

43

43a

43-43a   The 1938 deliveries were complemented by 10 further Leyland TD5s with very curvacious Northern Counties all-metal bodies (269-78). The interior decor was particularly attractive. Window surrounds were of stainless steel with polished wood and lower deck ceilings were covered in buff leather cloth, fading to blue at each side. No. 272 is shown loading for Moreton Shore at Woodside after the introduction of external advertisements in July 1946 as an additional source of revenue. No. 270 is coupled to the radiator heating equipment in Laird Street yard. Route number 7 was used for depot journeys on the Oxton Circle (via Borough Road) No. 6 service.
R H G Simpson/TG Turner collection

44-44a   The final pre-war delivery of new buses in 1939 comprised 40 Leyland Titan TD5c's with very attractive Massey bodies with similar interior features to the 1938 buses. They replaced a lesser number of Titan TD1s, the balance being used for expansion. Whilst echoing the curves of the Northern Counties designs, the lines were more restrained; the cream bands were edged with polished mouldings. Although supplied with torque-convertors, they had all been fitted with clutches and gear-boxes by 1950. Bus 288 stands at Stanley Lane, Eastham, the southern limit of normal service operations while 302 is seen in 1955 on the newly-introduced 70A service to Woodchurch Estate. Note the unusual way of displaying the route number.

T.Lawson/ J.W. Hughes

45 Laird Street depot received a direct hit in the air raids of March 1941. Many buses were seriously damaged though losses were minimised by dispersing part of the fleet to Birkenhead Park, a source of annoyance to residents of Cavendish Road. The tangled wreckage is bus No. 235, a 1937 Titan TD5c which, with a new Massey body, re-entered service in 1942. Six London Transport buses were hired to help out after the air raid losses but none was apparently photographed in Birkenhead.
Courtesy T.G. Turner

46 A post-war line up of buses at Woodside with the railway station in the background. Following introduction of the Formation of Queues Order in 1942, these islands with tubular metal shelters (effective only against vertical rain!) were erected so as to separate passengers for different routes. The official estimate of £800 for this work is hard to believe. Although displaying the destination 'Lower Bebington', No. 58 indicates that bus 215 is going on to Clatterbridge, an extension made in January 1946, though some workers' buses had run before that. Behind, No. 301 and a 1937 bus are going opposite ways round the Oxton Circle, No. 6 clockwise and No. 2 anti-clockwise.
R Marshall

47 The dock bridges and railway shunting operations caused many delays to the cross-docks joint services. A somewhat battered 240 is preceded by bus 352 in an experimental dark blue livery bound for Laird Street depot and a Wallasey bus en route to Charing Cross on route 11.
N.N. Forbes

48 The replacement bodies built by East Lancs. Coachbuilders in 1942 showed features of the pre-war Massey bodies. They were remarkable in not being built to the wartime utility standards. In 1949, all the rebodied buses were given new fleet numbers at the end of the series to avoid having to renumber them later if the numbers of new buses 'caught up'. No. 358 shown here was originally No. 206. It was working route 23 to Hurrell Road, a part-way route on the Moreton services 21-22.
R. Marshall

49

49a **49-49a**   During the war, the supply of new buses was controlled by the Ministry of Supply which allocated them on the basis of war workers' needs. Bodies were angular so that semi-skilled labour could be used and seats were of wood slats. Birkenhead received 36, all on Guy Arab chassis with 5-cylinder Gardner 5LW engines, though the last 12 (343-54) were delivered in 1946 and built to the 'relaxed' utility standard with rounded domes, upholstered seats and full destination equipment. The first utility bus, 319, delivered in September 1943, with Weymann body, is seen in original condition at Woodside except that it is in normal blue paint instead of its original wartime grey. Later it was converted to a breakdown vehicle, the upper deck being used for tree-cutting. It replaced No. 183 and lasted in this role until March 1968.
R Marshall/T.G. Turner collection

50

50a

50-50a   In all, four bodybuilders supplied bodies for the Guys - Weymann (2), Massey (18), Park Royal (12) and Northern Counties (4) and there were subtle differences in styling. Massey-bodied 326 of 1944 loads for Thurstaston with the now long gone Mersey Railway power station chimney in the background. Park Royal-bodied 346 of 1946 shows a noticeably more upright rear profile as it leaves the Library stop on Borough Road on the long Moreton-Bromborough route.

R Marshall/T.G. Turner collection

51

51a

51-51a   Wartime bodies did not wear well having usually been built using unseasoned timber and the Guys originally numbered 323-37 were rebodied with new 7 ft 9 in Massey bodies and fitted with new Gardner 6-cylinder 6LW engines in 1953. They were renumbered 241-55 and continued in service until 1969. One (242) has been preserved. These pictures show 247 (ex-329) crossing the Four Bridges in 1964 on a diversion when Duke Street bridge was closed and 246 (ex-328) late at night at Cross Lane, Bebington, on 24th November 1969, just before withdrawal.
T.G. Turner//T.G. Turner

52

52-52a The first new post-war buses, other than the Guys, were virtually identical to those delivered in 1939 except for the larger Leyland Titan PD1 radiator and sliding instead of half-drop windows. Fleet numbers reverted to 101 and 126 of 1948 is seen loading outside Sturla's Corner House, Hamilton Street, long demolished to accommodate tunnel approach roads. Note the stop signs of a design which first appeared in 1943 when stops were segregated to facilitate queuing. Note the modified paint-scheme with Gill-Sans letters and numbers which was introduced in the 1950s, 'Corporation' being omitted from the title after the merger of the bus and ferries departments as 'Birkenhead Municipal Transport' in 1953. Number 113 has run up Cole Street to unload in Grange Road West prior to moving on to the stand in Atherton Street used by the Wallasey services at Charing Cross.
Leyland/T.G. Turner

52a

53-53a At the end of the war the remaining 1930 Lions were in such a poor condition that sometimes there was no bus available to work the 44 service which was restricted to single-deck vehicles by the low bridge in Bromborough Road until Spital Road was made suitable for buses in 1965. These four Leyland PS1 buses with 33-seat Massey bodies arrived in June 1948 and were numbered 97-100. ACM 106 was originally allocated to No. 97 but the number had also been given to a motor cycle so it had to be renumbered ACM 194 as shown. Two of the four are seen at Liverpool Pier Head on hire to Crosville for the North Wales coastal express services.

T.G. Turner/RHG Simpson

53

53a

54   Transport management was impressed with the performance of the Gardner engines fitted to the wartime Guys and, as Leyland did not offer the Gardner as an option, placed orders for Guys and Daimlers in the post-war years. Seen standing at the Birch Road terminus of what had, in times past, been known as the 'Shopping Bus' is 1949 Guy Arab 151 with Massey body, on 4th June 1962, the day on which the route was renumbered from 79 to 97 so that 79 could be used for a new Prenton Dell Estate service. Note the absence of traffic on what is now a very busy road.
T.G. Turner

55

55-55a   Two batches each of 15 Daimlers CVG6s were delivered in 1949-50 (Nos. 161-90), all with Massey bodywork. Number 174 of 1949 turns from Arrowe Park Road into Arrowe Brook Road on the Woodside-Greasby service with Arrowe House Farm, now demolished, in the background while 181 of 1950 stands in Virginia Road, New Brighton on the No. 11 service to Higher Tranmere. Note that the latter retains the old style shaded title but with Gill Sans numerals.
TG Turner/R. Marshall

55a

56

56a

56-56a In 1951, Birkenhead got its first 8 ft wide buses - 20 Leyland PD2/3 buses with 57-seat bodies by Leyland, the first bodies by this manufacturer for 19 years - and the last as Leyland gave up bodybuilding soon after. The scenes are Woodchurch Estate in 1966 with 214 leaving the lay-by near Ackers Road with Daimler Fleetline 105 behind and Moreton Road, Upton with 215 on a diversion via Warwick Road during road works on Saughall Massie Road. Fleetline 103 is crossing into Arrowe Park Road.

A. Murray-Rust, courtesy T.G. Turner/T.G. Turner

57 Leyland PD2/3 No. 218 replaced Guy 319 as the towing-vehicle in 1968 and is seen recovering a training bus after the trainee lost control on New Chester Road, Bromborough during road works.
T.G. Turner

58

58a

58-58a There were further deliveries of Guy buses in 1950 and 1952. Massey-bodied 194 of 1950 passes Moss Lane, Prenton on the Woodchurch Estate service in 1959 while 58-seat East Lancs. bodied 237 crosses Hamilton Square. Note the old tramway standard and the crane involved in the erection of the Treasury Building.
T.G. Turner/T.G. Turner

59   The 1954 bodywork order for 15 Leyland PD2/12 buses was split between Weymann (10) and a local firm, Ashcroft (5). These are believed to have been the only bus bodies built by Ashcroft and No. 270 is seen at New Ferry Toll Bar, with the depot in the background, working the South Circle. The latter which started in 1946 was an extension of the Prenton service, traversing a long loop via Broadway, Kings Lane, Highfield Road, New Chester Road, Bebington Station and Town Lane. The Ashcroft bodies are believed to have incorporated Metal Sections framework; they had polished wood window interior mouldings and all but one continued in service until 1973.
AE Jones

60   Weymann-bodied 257, a 1954 Leyland PD2/12, turns from Borough Road into Whetstone Lane in November 1969. Note the old Fire Station and other buildings now rased to the ground. The street lamps are still mounted on tramway standards last used in regular service in 1906!
T.G. Turner

61 The original Upton terminus was in Salacre Lane but when the first by-pass (now part of Arrowe Park Road) was opened in 1938, buses stood on the new road, approaching via Rake Lane. Leyland PD2/12 362 with 59-seat East Lancs. body, new in 1955, is seen in Rake Lane on 23rd June 1964, the day after the 51 service from Port Sunlight was extended to Upton and Saughall Massie. After Merseyside PTE took over the buses in 1969, these buses (362-6) were transferred to Wallasey to replace older buses.
T.G. Turner

62

62a

62b

62-62a/b   The last Guy Arab buses were delivered in 1955-56. The 1955 order, with Massey bodies similar to those fitted to the rebuilt wartime buses, introduced a variation to the livery, the cream waist band being omitted and the title 'Birkenhead Transport' being placed on the lower panels either side of the municipal crest. Bus 355 is seen in Prenton Hall Road on the Prenton Circle, formed by joining up the 79 and 80 services in October 1965. The 1955 bodywork order was split between East Lancs.(5) and Massey (10) and Massey-bodied 374 is seen in Hamilton Square in 1965. East Lancs.-bodied 386, standing at Moreton Shore on route 87, New Ferry-Moreton Shore which ran only in the summers of 1960-62, had the distinction of carrying the highest fleet number of any Birkenhead bus.
A. Murray-Rust, courtesy T.G. Turner/T.G. Turner/T.G. Turner

63 From 1957, fleet numbers went back to No. 1, not used since the first municipal bus was withdrawn in 1927, and, for the next few years, Birkenhead Corporation standardised on Leyland PD2/40 buses with Massey bodywork, placing 15 new buses in service each year. Bus No. 1 is shown after transfer to Merseyside PTE who initially adopted a Wirral Division livery combining Birkenhead blue with Wallasey cream. Note that 'Road' has been painted out on the destination blind, following diversion of the service into Prenton Dell estate.
R.L. Wilson

64 Leyland PD2/40s appear identical and reflect the degree of standardisation as they were delivered seven years apart, 20 in 1959 and 128 in 1966. The seating capacity of the Massey bodywork had been increased to 66 by 1966. The picture was taken at Woodside on 24th April 1970 when Crosville crews staged a one day strike. Thus the Birkenhead crews refused to run to Eastham and the usual 39 service was curtailed to Manor Road as 38. No. 20 was the first ex-Birkenhead bus to be repainted in the Merseyside PTE livery.
T.G. Turner

65 Bus 62 was one of 30 Leyland PD2/40s with Massey body delivered between July 1962 and December 1963 and has turned from Hamilton Street into Conway Street soon after delivery. Note Sturla's Corner House and the old Market Hall in the background. All these buildings were later demolished to accommodate tunnel traffic.
T.G. Turner

66

66-67 In 1964 the Leyland Tiger PS1s were replaced by four underfloor-engined Leyland Leopard L1s with 42-seat dual entrance Massey bodies. The convention of numbering the single-deck buses in the nineties was retained and these vehicles became 91-4. Bus 93 is seen in Mill Park Drive on a special working of route 44 when new. After this route was diverted via Spital Road to avoid the low bridge at Trafalgar, these buses were transferred from New Ferry depot to Laird Street to work routes 12, Seacombe-Charing Cross and 97 Woodside-Oxton Village as one-man vehicles and 93 is seen in Hamilton Street in PTE livery on the latter route, by that time renumbered once again to 87. Note the market building now replaced by new municipal offices.
T.G. Turner/J. Manly

67

68 In 1962-63 Birkenhead Corporation tested three different rear-engined double-deck buses, two Leyland Atlanteans and a Daimler Fleetline and duly chose the latter, perhaps because the engineers liked the Gardner 6LX power unit. Nine 77-seat front-entrance Fleetlines (101-9) entered service in 1964, mainly for use on the busy Woodchurch Road services. They were delivered in a simplified livery - all blue with cream lower deck window surrounds (as on No. 107 seen working route 77) but were later repainted in the style carried by No. 108 which was working a Woodside-Arrowe Park short journey when this picture was taken in April 1968.
T.G. Turner

69 Pedestrians explore the Conway Street flyover on 13th July 1969, the day before it opened to traffic. Below, traffic in both directions uses the south carriageway, including 1965 PD2 123 on the Oxton Circle.
T.G. Turner

70 The later Massey-bodied Titans had a more upright front profile, necessary to accommodate their 66 seats and the lower deck side panels were vertical instead of curved at the bottom, a Massey feature designed to make some body parts interchangeable with Atlanteans. Bus 126 was approaching Duke Street bridge on a wet January day in 1967. *A.E. Jones*

71 A wintry scene on Ford Hill in February 1969 featured bus 142, one of the last traditional vertical-engined buses to be purchased by Birkenhead Corporation. It was a Leyland Titan PD2/37 with 66-seat Massey body. *P. Anderson*

72

72a

72-72a Birkenhead's first Leyland Atlantean PDR1/1s arrived in 1968. Massey had been taken over by Northern Counties Motor Engineering but the bodies were built in the Massey works. In 1969 eight of the 13 buses (155-67) were equipped for one-man operation and used on the Oxton Circle which was Birkenhead's first one-man operated double-deck route, converted on 3rd November 1969. The almost all blue livery was very drab, being designed for economical painting rather than elegance. No. 157 is seen on the parking ground at Woodside with the old landing stage just visible in the background while 160 leaves the market stop in Hamilton Street en route for the Woodchurch Estate.
T.G. Turner

73-73a The second 15 Atlanteans had front entrances and centre exits, features considered necessary at the time for successful one-man double-deck operation. The paint scheme on the Northern Counties bodies was much more attractive than on the previous delivery. Five of these buses were not delivered until after the PTE had taken over. Number 175 is seen in Laird Street yard when new while 182 stands in Boundary Road, New Ferry on 18th March 1973 without insignia. This became the terminus of route 10 to New Brighton after New Ferry depot closed. Most, if not all, these buses were transferred to work in Liverpool from Garston depot in 1979-80.
T.G. Turner/G.Parry

73

73a

74 After the New Ferry trams had been withdrawn on 27th December 1931, the depot which dated back to horse tramway days, was demolished and a garage for 50 buses was built very quickly on the site. It was also used as a bus station for the routes which terminated there. Wallasey Leyland PD2/12 No. 77 of 1952 and Birkenhead PD2/40 No. 35 of 1960 stand in the exit on 29th July 1969. The depot was closed as an economy measure on 3rd March 1973 and the post office and other buildings now occupy the site.

TG Turner

75

75a

75-75a   Birkenhead Corporation had ordered a further 13 dual-entrance Atlanteans which were not delivered until after Merseyside PTE had taken over in 1970. They were numbered 183-95 in the Birkenhead series and 194 is seen outside Exchange Station, Liverpool on the Liverpool-New Brighton service, the first regular daytime under-river bus service which commenced on 28th June 1971 using the Wallasey tunnel. The whole batch was fitted with step-counters for census taking and 193-4 were converted to single door layout as shown in this 1981 view when they were awaiting sale. By then they were in the PTE's verona green and jonquil livery.

N.N. Forbes/R.L.Wilson

76-76a   Single-deck Atlanteans were rare but Birkenhead Corporation had ordered two with 40-seat dual-door Northern Counties bodies which were delivered to the PTE in 1970, bearing numbers 95-6. They entered service in blue and cream livery but in November 1975 they were transferred to Liverpool and painted verona green. Number 95 is seen working on the special Railride service between Liverpool Central Station and James Street during construction work on the Loop line. Later they were transferred, together with Leopards 92-4 to Southport, where the same bus is seen in Lord Street on a local service, still with Birkenhead style destination indicators.
N.N. Forbes/R.L.Wilson

76a

77   In 1973-74 most of the Wirral bus routes were converted to one-man operation. However the rear-entrance Birkenhead buses were unsuitable so Atlanteans - some new and others ex-Liverpool Corporation were brought to Birkenhead and no fewer than 99 ex-Birkenhead Corporation double-deck buses were transferred to Liverpool and St. Helens, mainly for peak-hour workers' services. The former 80, renumbered L371 in the Liverpool series is seen at Regent Road, Seaforth in June 1973, repainted in Liverpool green. Ex-Birkenhead 61 and 147, converted to service vehicles, lasted long enough to be acquired by Merseybus in October 1986.
N.N. Forbes

78 Cross-river transfers were not all one way as two ex-Liverpool Corporation Leyland Royal Tiger buses were transferred to Laird Street in April 1970. They were painted blue, numbered 97-8 and worked as one-man buses on routes 12, 45 and 97. Bus 97 is seen leaving New Ferry depot for Brookhurst Estate, Bromborough in November 1970.
G. Parry

79 Many Liverpool-style Leyland Atlanteans worked in Birkenhead for Merseyside PTE but the 50 Daimler Fleetlines with Gardner 6LXB engines and Metropolitan-Cammell-Weymann 75-seat bodies, which went into service in 1973 (3001-50) spent all their service with the PTE in Wirral. Number 3044, bearing a short-lived simplified logo, is seen at Woodside on the peak hour Rapidride service 441 to Mill Park Estate in 1976. These buses were delivered in a dark blue and pale lemon livery which was eventually replaced by verona green. Buses 3011-20 spent some time working for Crosville at Heswall. All the Fleetlines were withdrawn in 1986 and some were then hired by Crosville to work in Liverpool.
R.L.Wilson

80

80a

80-80a   Leyland Lion 131, new in 1930, was converted as shown to take part in the Victory celebrations at the end of the 1939-45 war. It was converted back to a service bus in November 1945 and was withdrawn in May 1948. For the Festival of Britain in 1951, Leyland Titan TD5 301, new in 1939, was converted to an illuminated bus with extra batteries. It never re-entered service and was scrapped in 1953.
Courtesy T.G. Turner

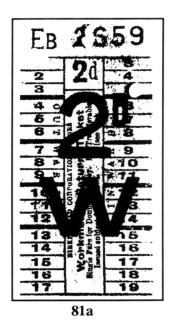

81a   **81b**   **81c**

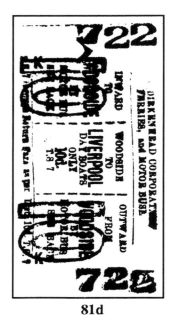

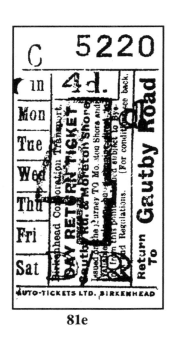

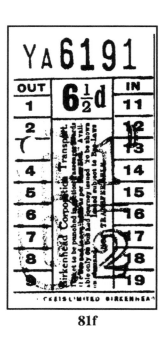

81d   **81e**   **81f**

Some Birkenhead tickets from bygone days.

81a   The ticket overprinted 2d W was a workmen's return, issued before 8.0am at single fare for the return journey. Birkenhead was particularly generous and allowed the return journey to be taken at any time over any correspondingly priced stage.

81b   A 3½d single ticket dating from the 1920s. Fares were reduced regularly during the early years so that, by 1931, some journeys cost only half the price charged ten years earlier.

81c   Although through tram or bus and ferry tickets had been issued for specific journeys from quite early in the century a comprehensive scheme was not put into operation until 1st April 1928, to combat reduced fares on the Mersey Railway. The 6d (2.5p) ticket, of which the ferries received 2½d (just over 1p), was available from Bebington Station, New Ferry Toll Bar, Prenton Dell Road, Noctorum Road and stages of similar length through to Liverpool Landing Stage, the equivalent, in some cases of a free ferry trip. Tickets ranged from 5d to 1/4d (6.7p) the latter from Heswall.

81d   The tickets issued at the ferry turnstiles were of the Edmondson card type as used by the railways.

81e   The Corporation sponsored various cheap tickets in the summer, designed to make trips to the country or the seaside affordable for the underprivileged. This 4d return was valid from Gautby Road to Moreton Shore and there was a range of cheap 6d returns to Arrowe Park.

81f   Fares were stable for 20 years until post-war inflation necessitated regular increases and this 6½d (about 3p) ticket dates from that time. Birkenhead's tickets were always printed by Auto-Tickets Ltd whose works was in Laird Street almost opposite the bus depot.

WOODSIDE AND PRENTON.

Via. **Chester Street, Central Station, Borough Road and Singleton Avenue.**

MONDAY TO FRIDAY

		a.m.	a.m.	a.m.	and every 10 mins until	a.m.	a.m.	then every 20 mins until	p.m.	and every 10 mins until	p.m.	then every 20 mins until	p.m.
Woodside	leave	7 40	8 0	8 10		10 0	10 20		4 0		7 20		11 0
Osmaston Rd.	arrive	7 58	8 18	8 28		10 18	10 38		4 18		7 38		11 18

SATURDAYS -										SUNDAYS		
		a.m.	a.m.	a.m.	a.m.	a.m.	a.m.	and every 10 mins. until	p.m.	p.m.	p.m.	then every 20 mins until	p.m.
Woodside	leave	7 40	8 0	8 10	8 20	8 30	8 40		11 0	1 0	1 20		11 0
Osmaston Rd.	arrive	7 58	8 18	8 28	8 38	8 48	8 58		11 18	1 18	1 38		11 18

PRENTON AND WOODSIDE.

Via. **Singleton Avenue, Borough Road, Central Station and Argyle Street.**

MONDAY TO FRIDAY

		a.m.	a.m	and every 10 mins. until	a.m.	a.m.	and every 20 mins. until	p.m.	then every 10 mins. until	p.m.	and every 20 mins. until	p.m.
Osmaston Rd.	leave	8 2	8 12		10 22	10 42		4 22		7 42		11 22
Woodside	arrive	8 18	8 28		10 38	10 58		4 38		7 58		11 38

SATURDAYS									SUNDAYS		
		a.m.	a.m.	a.m.	a.m.	a.m.	and every 10 mins. until	p.m.	p.m.	p.m.	and every 20 mins. until	p.m.
Osmaston Rd.	leave	8 2	8 12	8 22	8 32	8 42		11 22	1 20	1 40		11 20
Woodside	arrive	8 18	8 28	8 38	8 48	8 58		11 38	1 38	1 58		11 38

SPECIAL NOTICE.—Buses leaving Woodside for Prenton between 4-0 and 7-0 p.m. Monday to Friday, and 12-0 noon and 2-0 p.m. on Saturday will accept only through passengers (for beyond Singleton Avenue) until reaching Whetstone Lane.

The above service is extended to Arrowe Park on Saturday Afternoons only (see below), leaving Woodside at 1-30 p.m and every 10 mins. until 8-50 p.m. and returning at 1-55 p.m. and every 10 min. until 9-15

BOY SCOUTS WORLD JAMBOREE

During the period of the above, a frequent service of Buses will be run between Woodside and Arrowe Park, also, if necessary, between Prenton Tram Terminus and Arrowe Park.

Taken from Birkenhead Corporation Tramways and Motors Timetables, August 1929.

SUMMARY OF BIRKENHEAD CORPORATION BUS FLEET 1919-70

Fleet No.	Registration No.	Chassis Make and Type	Body Make	Type & Capacity	Year in Service	Year Withdrawn	Notes
1-10	CM 1701-10	Leyland 'O'	Leyland	B32R	1919-20	1927	
11-2	CM 1711-2	AEC 'B'	LGOC	O16/18R	1921	1925-6	A
13-5	CO 3398-400	Straker Squire 'A'	Straker Squire	B32R	1922	1927	B
16	CM 4006	Straker Squire 'A'	Straker Squire	B32R	1922	1927	C
17	CM 4686	Thornycroft BT	Strachan & Brown	B20F	1923	1928	
18-23	CM 4936-41	Leyland G7	Leyland	B32R	1923	1928-9	
24-9	CM 5339-44	Leyland SGH7	Leyland	FB40R	1924	1930	
30-2	CM 5345-7	Leyland Leviathan LG1	Leyland	H28/24RO	1925	1930	
33-7	CM 6040-4	Leyland Leviathan LG1	Leyland	H28/24RO	1925	1930	
38	CM 6045	Guy 'J'	Buckingham	B20F	1925	1930	
39-41	CM 6046-8	Leyland SG11	Leyland	B36R	1925	1931	
42-3	CM 6049-50	Leyland Leviathan LG1	Leyland	H26/26RO	1926	1931	
44-51	CM 6600-7	Leyland Leviathan LG1	Leyland	H26/26RO	1926	1931	
52-4	CM 6608-10	Guy 'BB'	Guy	B27D	1926	1930	
55-64	CM 6611-20	Leyland Leviathan LSP2	Leyland	H28/27R	1927	1933	
65-74	CM 7384-93	Leyland PLSC3	Leyland	B36R	1927-8	1935	
75-8	CM 8060-3	Leyland PLSC3	Leyland	B36R	1928	1935	
79-93	CM 8064-78	Leyland Titan TD1	Leyland	L27/24RO	1928	1938	D
94-113	CM 8721-40	Leyland Titan TD1	Leyland	L24/24R	1929-30	1939	
114-25	CM 9375-86	Leyland Titan TD1	Leyland	L24/24R	1930	1939-44	
126-31	CM 9387-92	Leyland Lion LT2	Leyland	B35R	1930	1939-48	
132-51	CM 9756-75	Leyland Titan TD1	Leyland	L27/24R	1930-31	1944-7	
152-6	BG 200-4	Leyland Titan TD1	Leyland	L27/24R	1931	1944-6	
157-8	BG 205-6	Daimler CH6	Massey	L27/26R	1931	1938	
159-63	BG 472-6	Leyland Titan TD1	Massey	L27/24R	1931	1944-7	
164-70	BG 739-45	Leyland Titan TD2	Leyland	L27/24R	1932	1940-8	
171-5	BG 746-50	Daimler CH6	Massey	L26/26R	1932	1938	
176-84	BG 1500-8	Leyland Titan TD2	Massey	L27/24R	1933	1947-8	E
185	BG 1509	AEC 'Q'	MCCW	L31/28F	1933	1940	
186-8	BG 2651-3	Leyland Titan TD3c	NCME	L26/24R	1934	1948-9	
189-91	BG 2654-6	Leyland Titan TD3c	NCME	H28/24R	1934	1948-9	
192-7	BG 2657-62	Leyland Titan TD3c	Massey	H28/24R	1934	1949	
198-202	BG 3423-7	Leyland Titan TD4c	Massey	H30/24R	1935	1949-52	F
203-7	BG 3428-32	Leyland Titan TD4c	NCME	H30/24R	1935	1949-52	F
208-18	BG 4381-91	Leyland Titan TD4c	Massey	H30/24R	1936	1949-52	G
219-58	BG 5501-40	Leyland Titan TD5c	Massey	H30/24R	1937	1950-1	H
259-68	BG 6801-10	Leyland Titan TD5c	Massey	H30/24R	1938	1950-1	
269-78	BG 6811-20	Leyland Titan TD5c	NCME	H30/24R	1938	1953-5	
279-318	BG 7701-40	Leyland Titan TD5c	Massey	H30/24R	1939	1951-7	
319-20	BG 8552-3	Guy Arab 5LW	Weymann	H30/26R	1943	1951-4	
321-25	BG 8554-8	Guy Arab 5LW	Massey	H30/26R	1943-4	1954-69	J
326-30	BG 8628-32	Guy Arab 5LW	Massey	H30/26R	1943-4	1954-69	J
331-8	BG 8641-8	Guy Arab 5LW	Massey	H30/26R	1943-4	1954-69	J
339-42	BG 8649-52	Guy Arab 5LW	Park Royal	H30/26R	1944	1954	
343-50	BG 8735-42	Guy Arab 5LW	Park Royal	H30/26R	1946	1957-9	
351-4	BG 8743-6	Guy Arab 5LW	NCME	H30/26R	1946	1957-9	
101-12	BG 9221-32	Leyland Titan PD1	Massey	H30/26R	1946	1959-60	
113-25	BG 9531-6 9672-8	Leyland Titan PD1	Massey	H30/26R	1947	1959-61	K
97-100	ACM 194,107-9	Leyland Tiger PS1	Massey	B33R	1948	1964	L
126-45	ACM 301-20	Leyland Titan PD1	Massey	H30/26R	1948	1961-3	
146-60	ACM 604-18	Guy Arab 6LW	Massey	H30/26R	1949	1962-3	
161-75	ACM 619-33	Daimler CVG6	Massey	H30/26R	1949	1963-5	
176-90	ABG 176-90	Daimler CVG6	Massey	H30/26R	1950	1964-6	
191-205	ABG 291-305	Guy Arab 6LW	Massey	H30/26R	1950	1965-6	
206-25	ABG 806-25	Leyland Titan PD2/3	Leyland	H31/26R	1951	1966-7	M
226-40	BCM 926-40	Guy Arab 6LW	East Lancs	H33/26R	1952	1968-9	

256-65	CBG 556-65	Leyland Titan PD2/12	Weymann	H33/26R	1954	1969-73		
266-70	CBG 566-70	Leyland Titan PD2/12	Ashcroft	H33/26R	1954	1972-3		
355-61	DCM 975-81	Guy Arab IV 6LW	Massey	H31/28R	1955	1972		
362-6	DCM 982-6	Leyland Titan PD2/12	East Lancs	H31/28R	1955	1973		
367-71	DCM 987-91	Leyland Titan PD2/12	Weymann	H33/26R	1955	1972-3		
372-7	EBG 59-64	Guy Arab IV 6LW	Massey	H31/28R	1956	1970-2		
378-81	EBG 750-3	Guy Arab 1V 6LW	Massey	H31/28R	1956	1970-2		
382-6	EBG 754-8	Guy Arab IV 6LW	East Lancs	H31/28R	1956	1971-2		
1-8	FCM 991-8	Leyland Titan PD2/40	Massey	H31/28R	1957-8	1972-3		
9-15	FBG 909-15	Leyland Titan PD2/40	Massey	H31/28R	1957-8	1973-4		
16-30	HCM 516-30	Leyland Titan PD2/40	Massey	H33/28R	1959-60	1974-5	N	
31-45	JBG 531-45	Leyland Titan PD2/40	Massey	H35/28R	1960-61	1973-4		
46-60	LCM 446-60	Leyland Titan PD2/40	East Lancs	H37/28R	1961	1973-4		
61-75	MCM 961-75	Leyland Titan PD2/40	Massey	H35/30R	1962	1973-5		
76-90	OCM 976-90	Leyland Titan PD2/40	Massey	H35/30R	1963	1975-5		
91-4	RCM 491-4	Leyland Leopard L1	Massey	B42D	1964	1974-7		
101-9	RCM 501-9	Daimler Fleetline CRG6LX	Weymann	H44/33F	1964	1977-8		
110-24	BBG 110-24C	Leyland Titan PD2/40	Massey	H36/30R	1965	1973-4		
125-39	DBG 125-39D	Leyland Titan PD2/40	Massey	H36/30R	1966	1973-4		
140-54	GCM 140-54E	Leyland Titan PD2/37	Massey	H36/30R	1967	1975-7		
155-67	LCM 155-67G	Leyland Atlantean PDR1/1	NCME	H44/33F	1968	1980-1		
168-82	MBG 368-82H	Leyland Atlantean PDR1/2	NCME	H44/27D	1969-70	1981	Some P	
183-95	OBG 383-95J	Leyland Atlantean PDR1A/1	NCME	H44/27D	1970	1981	P	
95-6	OBG 495-6J	Leyland Atlantean PDR2/1	NCME	B40D	1970	1981	P	

KEY TO BODY TYPE CODE

B = Saloon Bus FB = Fully fronted saloon bus H = Highbridge type double deck L - Lowbridge type double deck O = Open top double deck.   Figures denote seating capacity - upper deck first.
Final letter denotes door position. F = Front R = Rear D = Dual RO = Rear, open staircase.

NOTES

A   Second hand from London General Omnibus Co.Ltd.
B   Second hand from Plymouth Corporartion
C   Second hand from W.B.Horn, Birkenhead
D   Rebuilt with enclosed stairs 1933.
E   182 damaged in air raid 1941; given new East Lancs H30/26R body in 1942; body transferred to 217 (356) in 1947.
     183 destroyed by fire in 1936; chassis used for a breakdown crane, in service until 1953.
F   198, 204 and 206 damaged in air raids 1941 and fitted with new East Lancs H30/26R bodies in 1942; renumbered 355, 357 and 358 in 1947-8.
G   214 fitted with new East Lancs H30/26R body in 1942; renumbered 359 in 1947.
     217 renumbered 356 in 1947 on receiving new body from 182.
H   226, 235 rebodied by Massey in 1942; renumbered 360-1 in 1947.
J   319 rebuilt as breakdown crane in 1951 and ran until 1968. 323-37 rebodied with new Massey 7ft9in bodies and fitted with 6LW engines 1953. Renumbered 241-55 and ran until 1969.
K   Registration and fleet numbers not in sequence.
L   97 was for a short time registered ACM106 in error.
M   First 8ft wide buses.
N   21-3, 25-30 transferred to Wallasey by PTE 1970 and renumbered 21-3B, 25-30B; renumbered 321-3, 325-30 in 1971.
P   Ordered by Birkenhead Corporation but delivered to Merseyside PTE.

All buses 1919-32 up to 168, 171-5 and 185 had petrol engines, all others diesel.

ACKNOWLEDGEMENTS

The pictures and information in this publication have been accumulated over many years and thanks are due to the many photographers for allowing their work to be published.

Special thanks are due to TG Turner whose profound knowledge of the Birkenhead bus undertaking has been freely shared with the author. Without his photographic work, it would have been impossible to give a comprehensive picture of this fine municipal undertaking.

David Thompson, Archivist, and the staff of Wirral Borough Libraries have given invaluable assistance in preserving old documents and making them available for inspection.

JN Barlow, JE Eaton, M Jenkins, GD Parry, KW Swallow, M Wallas and F Woodland also contributed invaluable information.

ABOUT THE AUTHOR

A native of Wallasey, the author's interest in public transport was evident before his third birthday when he screamed loudly when taken in his pushchair on to the promenade where there were no trams or buses! His first job was with the LMS Railway in the Birkenhead Goods department where he was parentally steered because "it was a safe job with a pension at the end of it". After transport-related army service he went into bus operation, eventually taking charge of the Ribble company's operations, first at Blackpool and then at Preston, the company's biggest depot at the time.

After secondment to the Merseyside Area Land Use and Transportation Study in 1966-67 he joined the United Transport group, serving in a number of African countries for twenty-two years. He returned to Wirral in 1992.

This is his 18th book, other transport books on local subjects being the acclaimed five-volume *Liverpool Transport* (with JB Horne), *The Tramways of Birkenhead and Wallasey* (with M Jenkins), *Mersey Ferries Vol. 1*, *Crosville on Merseyside* and *Motor Coach Services from Merseyside*.